Greencombe
A poem in paths

ELLA DUFFY

HAZEL PRESS

First published in 2024
by Hazel Press Publishers
22 Coneygar Close, Bridport, Dorset DT6 3AR
www.hazelpress.co.uk

Text copyright © Ella Duffy 2024
Cover image copyright © John Hurford 2024 and Rob Schmidt 2024

All rights reserved. No part of this publication may be reproduced in any form or by any means without the prior permission of the publisher.

A CIP record for this title is available from the British Library

Design/typography: Dale Tomlinson
Typeface: Mrs Eaves (designed by Zuzana Licko)
Cover: Details from the right and left sides of *The Greencombe Triptych*, by John Hurford (2009). With thanks to Rob Schmidt of Greencombe Gardens.

ISBN 978-1-7394218-4-7

First Edition

Printed in England by Anglian Print Ltd, Beccles, Suffolk, on 100% recycled paper, using vegetable-based inks. Anglia Print has gained the following certifications:

for Daphne

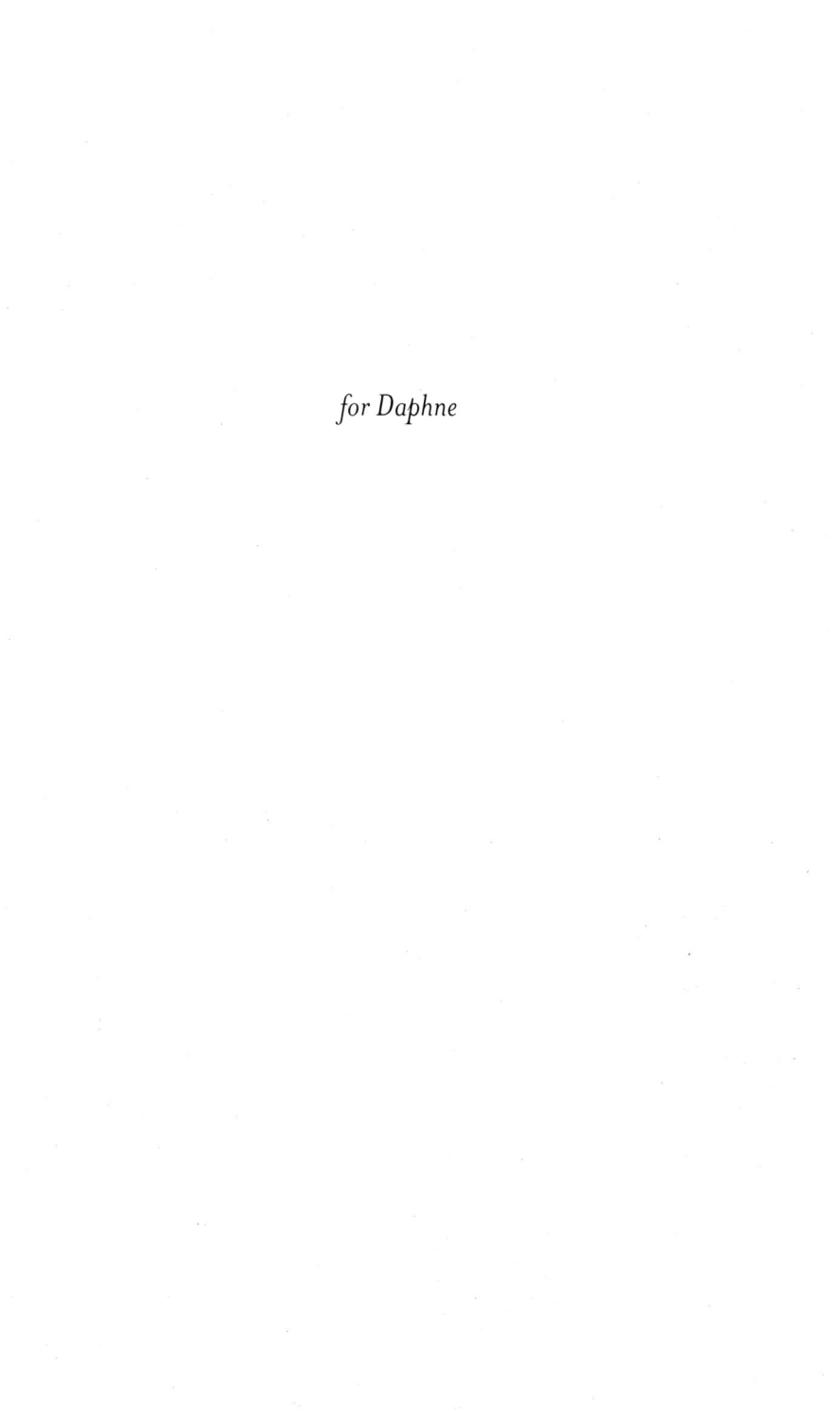

Contents

underway — 7
top path — 8
ravine — 8
lower drive — 9
first path up — 10
great holly circle — 10
top path — 11
main path — 12
water channel — 12
badger path — 13
squirrel path — 13
jay walk/hop — 14
snail crawl — 15
keyhole — 15
barrow's path — 16
owl's path — 17
bottom path — 17
weasel walk — 18
the gut — 19
short cut — 20
bottom path — 21
chapel steps — 21
bottom path — 22
main path — 22
hare path — 23
mouse path — 24
deer path — 25
fox path — 25
protistum way — 26

Map of the Gardens at Greencombe — 29
John Hurford, psychedelic artist — 30
Joan Loraine and Greencombe Gardens — 31

--------- underway

Consistent rain has churned the path.
Further on, the clouds part for magnolia.

- - - - - - - - - - top path

Shed, fruit cage, huddle of pots.
A kitchen garden; herb-measured, veg-tied.
Through an arch in the wall, the path changes
from brick to soil to stone.

- - - - - - - - - - ravine

Stone steps. Grass.
Then down the dip
to a small raised pond.
A backswimmer with hair-slick legs
completes its upended lap.

- - - - - - - - - lower drive

A larger pond, edged
with old quarry stone,
reflects new light.
To your right, the first Guardian Oak.
Dream of this tree for a long life.
Stand at the lookout.
Ahead, the saltmarsh.
Years back, the sea rose
and breached the shingle ridge,
petrified the trees.
From where you stand, the forest
is a distant stillness.

- - - - - - - - - first path up

Dry stone wall. Black iron gate.
First path up, bridled with camellias.

- - - - - - - - - great holly circle

Shallow steps to the holly.
Coppiced, it grew multiple trunks.
A long burred life.
The path cuts through, circles back.
This is the first time you've walked
through the centre of a tree.
Ahead, four centuries of ghosts
walking the same circular route.

- - - - - - - - - - top path

What kind of moss is this?
Round tuft; river-green.
Upright stems; red-brown.
Swan's neck moss.
Hold it as you might an injured bird.

- - - - - - - - - - main path

You've walked through gardens
where a bench is an invitation
to face out towards a further view.
Behind you, the garden engaged in a game
of grandmother's footsteps;
slow creep of plant-life,
all the insects lifting their feet.
Here, the benches face inwards.
To rest is to turn to the garden.

- - - - - - - - - - water channel

Path of stones doing the work of a stream.
Rain wakes the stone from its hard sleep,
slicks it alive. Grey-quick; it tricks
the light to the shape of an otter.

- - - - - - - - - badger path

Watch and wander. Walk
this downward path,
past the four-faced bed.
Eye of spore; of wing;
of bark; of seed.

- - - - - - - - - squirrel path

What grows in acidic soil?
Azaleas, pink
to jumpstart a thought.

- - - - - - - - - jay walk/hop

Left foot, right foot.
Jay walk, jay hop.
Bird wing, bird foot.
Three-oak bed
with acorns
for the jay to store
understones
underground.
One bird can bury
three-thousand
acorns a month.
Blue-dipped feather
on the path.
Bird wing, bird foot.
Jay walk, jay hop.
Left foot, right foot.

- - - - - - - - - snail crawl

The slight downhill
flusters your step.
Small stones, kicked up.
Clack of empty snail shell;
its weight, an absence.

- - - - - - - - - - keyhole

Detour: a path
designed to ease
the flow of gardenwork.
To your right, the second Guardian.
To your left, the third.
For two months of the year
the sun refuses to sit up from behind its hill.
Only catkins candle the hours.

- - - - - - - - - barrow's path

What needs doing?
Thirty tons of leaf-mould and compost
made and used each year.
Bacteria-written, worm-gripped.
The earth's book is shelved in this garden.

- - - - - - - - - owl's path

A farmer, herding sheep in the lower field,
calls with long vowels.
At night, the tawny owl shepherds the dark.
A lower pitch to push through
the dense standing of trees.

- - - - - - - - - bottom path

You pass the next three Guardian Oaks;
their long lines and invisible lines
work to pull your head up and back
as if you were a marionette.
When the strings tangle,
one foot trips over the other.
The hinge in your ankle creaks.

– – – – – – – – – weasel walk

Something irresistible about a narrow path,
like a hushed secret; you lean in.

- - - - - - - - - - the gut

Medieval ditch, dug
from the lowest section of the wood.
Cut into the bank, three leaf stores.
After midsummer, old leaves
will be turned. A scattering of wood ash
to urge things along.
When the leaf-mould is ready,
it's best spread thick.
Black butter. Slow melt.

- - - - - - - - - - short cut

To where?
To what?

--------- bottom path

The garden
has thrown itself
up into the air
and is growing
vertically.
Feet still
but eyes quick,
you take in
over a hundred trees.

---------- chapel steps

The walls, chestnut.
The roof, pine.
The sculpture, chestnut
standing on oak.
For those who pray,
the chapel is its own wood.

- - - - - - - - - bottom path

Moving east along the moss:
a tiered bed of erythronium,
a guarding of dog's-tooth violet.
Stems thin. Petals held mid-dive.
Later, a tree stump
the shape of a fallen star.

- - - - - - - - - main path

A parallel self walks west
along the main path.
You starcross, unaware.

- - - - - - - - - - hare path

Four chestnuts
open four doors.
A hare bolts
from the underworld.

- - - - - - - - - - mouse path

On the other side of the door,
the garden narrows and cools.
The woodsedge has rushed
to fill each greenless gap.
Flowers like snow; settling, settling.
No longer a path, but a space
only a mouse could pass through.

- - - - - - - - - - deer path

Moss-drum. Lichen-snare.
In this garden, on this path,
you are a fawn, newly listening.
Beetles clickclick in the leaf-fall.
A twig splits underfoot.

- - - - - - - - - - fox path

Or like a cub, newly scenting.
Petrichor; the perfume
the earth puts on
to meet the rain.

- - - - - - - - - - protistum way

The air above the sea rotates.
It rains and spins the garden
on its axis. You shelter
beneath a rhododendron;
the largest you've ever seen.
Leaves the size of roof tiles;
you are standing in a room
generous with light.
Your presence here, only addition.

The Gardens at Greencombe

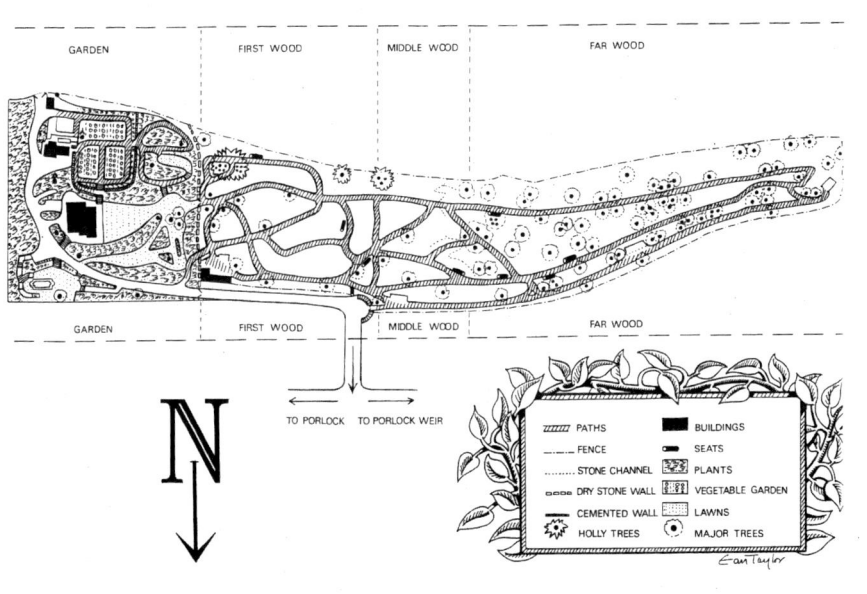

GARDEN	FIRST WOOD	MIDDLE WOOD	FAR WOOD

TO PORLOCK   TO PORLOCK WEIR

N

- PATHS
- FENCE
- STONE CHANNEL
- DRY STONE WALL
- CEMENTED WALL
- HOLLY TREES
- BUILDINGS
- SEATS
- PLANTS
- VEGETABLE GARDEN
- LAWNS
- MAJOR TREES

John Hurford, psychedelic artist

The cover of this book features details from the *Greencombe Triptych*, painted by the veteran 1960s' psychedelic artist and Devon farmer John Hurford.

John made his name illustrating for *Oz*, *Gandalf's Garden* and *International Times* and by designing book and album covers. His work is crowded with highly detailed observations of the natural world.

'When I arrived for the first time at Greencombe on an April morning I was shocked by what I saw. I had imagined a large cottage garden with a few borders and a few flowering shrubs, but the reality was overpowering. The variety of the plants, the sheer size of the garden, the colours and the smells.

'Every so often you come across an example of someone's lifetime work; the result of them steadfastly following their own particular personal passion. The life's work I saw in the spring of 2007 was a garden.'

Greencombe and Joan Loraine

Greencombe is a woodland garden of mazy paths, tucked below the north slopes of Porlock Hill on Exmoor. From November to February, the sun fails to reach over the hill and the land waits in shadow. It faces the bay and a mercurial stretch of water described as a 'sunless sea' in Coleridge's visionary poem *Kubla Khan*. In summer, the garden unfurls into an otherworldly sunny paradise.

Plantswoman Joan Loraine (1924–2016) developed Greencombe over 50 years. When she arrived in 1966, there was only a thin layer of soil. Every autumn she gathered fallen leaves to make leaf mould, from which she made an enriching mulch to spread in the spring, a process that continues today.

The garden contains four National Plant Collections:

- Erythronium (small woodland and mountain lilies)
- Polystichum (the thumbs-up fern)
- Vaccinium (includes cranberry, blueberry and Exmoor's whortleberry)
- Gaultheria (berries for bears)